LET'S TALK CLIMATE CHANGE

TAKE ACTION

BE POSITIVE

LOVE OUR PLANET

by Ruth Owen

Ruby Tuesday Books

Published in 2026 by Ruby Tuesday Books Ltd.

Editor: Mark J. Sachner

Design & Production: Alix Wood, Elaine Wilkinson, & Tammy West

With thanks to:
Dr. Alex Standish
Senior Lecturer in Geography Education
University College London, UK

Picture Credits:

Character illustrations by Lemono (Shutterstock).

Alamy: 17T (All Canada Photos), 26B (Zuma Press Inc); ATS Energy: 23BR; ESA: 18B; James Kuether: 7T; NASA: 14B; National Science Foundation (Heidi Roop/David Noone): 19T; NOAA: 7B; Science Photo Library: 18T (Simon Fraser), 24B (E.R. Degginger); Shutterstock: 5 (Vaclav Volrab/Rifrazione_foto), 6L (O.C. Ritz), 6R (Allison H. Smith), 8C, 8B, 9 (Vector Mine), 10 (Happy Job/Lana Brow), 11T (elenabsl/Ivanov Ksenia/Sky and glass), 11B (3d_man), 12TR (Budimir Jevtic), 12B (Jakinnboaz), 13BL (Charles Bowman), 13BR, 14T (titoOnz), 15TL (titoOnz), 15TR (Steve Allen), 16T (GTW), 16B (Danita Delimont), 17C (Leonid S. Shtandel), 19B (Graphic Farm), 22T (Andrea Danti), 22B (Macrovector), 23T (petovarga), 23C, 23BL (Dominik Gajda), 24T (Bilanol), 24B (Good Dreams Studio/Montree Nanta), 25C, 25B (Damsea), 26T (Korawat photo shoot), 26C (sociologas/corund/New Africa), 27TR (Lightspring), 27TL (Damsea), 27CR (riezart), 27BR (Smirnov Vladimir), 31T (Simone Hogan).

Library of Congress Control Number: 2025946371

Print (Hardback) ISBN 978-1-78856-639-1

Print (Paperback) ISBN 978-1-78856-640-7

ePub ISBN 978-1-78856-641-4

Published in Minneapolis, MN

Printed in the United States

www.rubytuesdaybooks.com

CONTENTS

Page 4
The BIG Questions

Page 6
What Is Climate and How Is It Changing?

Page 8
Why Is Earth Getting Warmer?

Page 10
Are Cell Phones Making Earth Warm Up?

Page 12
What Are the Effects of Climate Change?

Page 14
Are the North and South Poles Melting?

Page 16
Will Climate Change Cause Animal Extinctions?

Page 18
How Do Scientists Study and Track Climate Change?

Page 20
How Do I Know What Information to Trust?

Page 22
Can We Still Power Our World While Making Fewer Greenhouse Gases?

Page 24
Can We Take Carbon Dioxide Out of the Air?

Page 26
Are There Other Ways to Reduce Greenhouse Gases?

Page 28
What Can I Do to Help?

Page 30
Is It Too Late to Fix Our Planet?

Page 32
Glossary and Index

The BIG Questions

Climate change is big news. So it's not surprising that we all have lots of questions.

What things are people doing to help stop climate change?

Will climate change hurt wild animals?

Is the world going to end?

What will our world be like when I'm older?

Why will hotter temperatures make the ocean rise?

Is global warming the same as climate change?

Is it too late to fix our planet?

What questions do you have about climate change?

It's completely normal to worry about this important subject.

The changes in Earth's climate are having big effects on the weather, the oceans, natural habitats, animals—and on people.

Every day we are bombarded with information—and sometimes it's scary!

But can we always trust everything we hear, see, and read?

TOP STORIES

By the end of this decade, polar bears will have nowhere to live.

Our planet is burning!

This book is all about answering climate change questions using scientific evidence.

It's also about the ways in which scientists, inventors, engineers, conservationists, entrepreneurs, politicians, and kids like you are taking positive action to help our wonderful planet.

Ready for a big discussion?

Let's Talk Climate Change

What Is Climate and How Is It Changing?

Climate is the usual weather and temperatures in an area, state, or even a whole country.

If you live in Phoenix, Arizona, the climate is dry with warm or hot weather all year round.

In Anchorage, Alaska, people live in a climate with freezing-cold, snowy winters.

Phoenix, Arizona

- Hottest summer temperatures of 100°F (38°C)
- Winter temperatures of 50° F (10°C)
- 3 inches (7.5 cm) of rain each year
- Hardly ever snows

Anchorage, Alaska

- Hottest summer temperature of 65°F (18°C)
- Winter temperature of 13°F (-10°C)
- About 100 inches (2.5 m) of snow each year

Are weather and climate different?

Yes! Weather is a rainy day, a hot, sunny week, or a cold, snowy month. It's what happens over a short period of time.

To describe an area's climate, scientists observe the weather and temperatures for about 30 years.

For example, it might rain in Phoenix, Arizona, for a few days—that's weather. But usually the climate in Phoenix is very dry.

Climate change is the way in which Earth's climate changes over time.

If we could travel back millions of years to the age of the dinosaurs, Earth's average temperature would be warmer than today. At other times, our planet has experienced freezing ice ages.

Warmer Times

Today, Antarctica is the coldest place on Earth. The whole continent is covered with thick ice. However, about 100 million years ago, Antarctica was home to warm forests of tall trees, ferns, and other plants.

Antarctica
100 million years ago

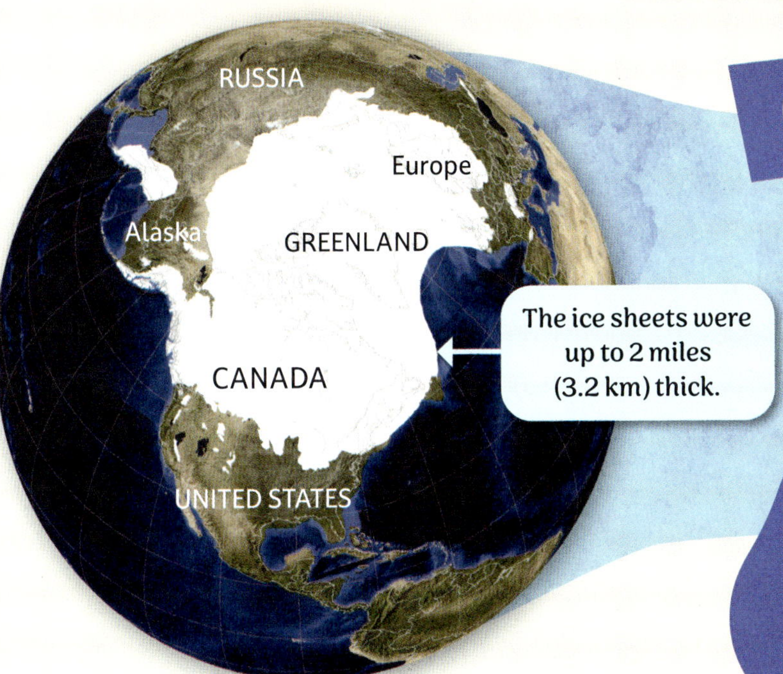

The ice sheets were up to 2 miles (3.2 km) thick.

Colder Times

The last ice age began about 1.8 million years ago. It ended about 10,000 years ago. During this time, large parts of Earth were covered with thick ice.

Past changes in Earth's climate happened slowly over thousands or millions of years.

Right now, our planet's climate is growing warmer. In the past 125 years, Earth's average temperature has risen by almost 2.2 degrees Fahrenheit (1.2 degrees Celsius).

It might seem that 125 years is a long time, but it's actually a very short period for so much warming to happen.

Why Is Earth Getting Warmer?

Earth is surrounded by a layer of gases called the atmosphere.

Some of the gases in the atmosphere are known as greenhouse gases.

Greenhouse gases make life on Earth possible by trapping heat from the Sun. Without them, Earth would freeze! However, in the past 125 years, there has been an increase in these gases in the atmosphere.

You might hear people call carbon dioxide "CO_2." That's its chemical symbol, or science name.

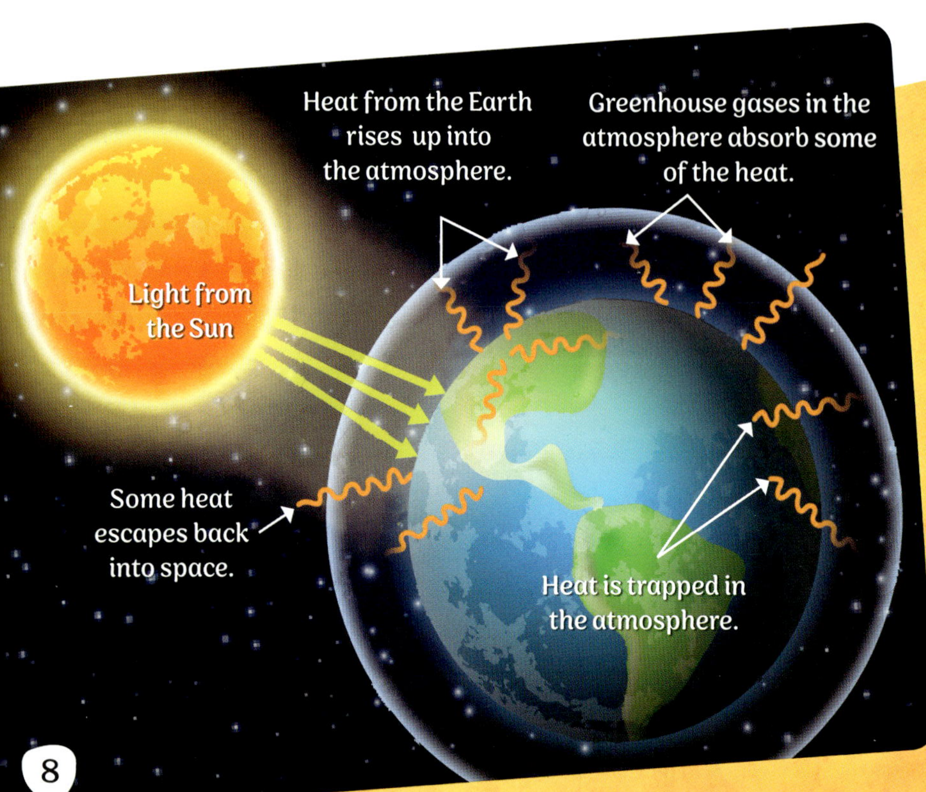

More gases mean more heat is trapped, making Earth grow warmer. This is called the greenhouse effect. It's similar to the way in which the glass of a greenhouse traps the Sun's heat inside.

Most scientists believe that Earth is warming up because of human actions.

For more than 150 years, people have been using coal, oil, and natural gas to create energy. These types of fuels are known as fossil fuels.

Vehicles, boats, and planes are powered by gasoline or diesel fuels that are made from oil.

Power plants burn coal and natural gas to make electricity.

Factories and farms use electricity, oil, coal, and natural gas to produce all the things we need.

Homes use natural gas for heating and cooking. They also use electricity.

Offices, schools, hospitals, and stores use electricity.

Rotting garbage at landfill sites releases greenhouse gases into the air.

The gradual warming of Earth is known as global warming.

When we burn fossil fuels to make energy, they release large amounts of carbon dioxide and other greenhouse gases into the air.

Are Cell Phones Making Earth Warm Up?

We use phones to stay in touch, keep safe, to do our jobs or schoolwork—and for FUN!

However, using phones creates huge amounts of some greenhouse gases.

To make phones, metals must be mined, or dug, from the ground. Glass and plastic must be produced. These processes use energy and create greenhouse gases.

We use electricity every day to charge our phones.

THE FACTORIES THAT BUILD PHONES USE ENERGY.

The ships and trucks that transport phones around the world burn fuel.

When we upgrade to a new phone, our old device may become e-waste buried in a landfill site. It can leak toxic chemicals into the ground and release gases into the air.

Tablets, laptops, and consoles create greenhouse gases in the same ways as our phones!

And all those photos, funny videos, messages, websites, and online games aren't actually just floating around in the clouds.

All this data is stored on computers in vast buildings called data centers.

Data centers use huge amounts of electricity to power the computers.

Computers inside a data center

And data centers get **VERY** hot! Even more energy is needed to power cooling systems to keep the buildings cool and prevent the computers from overheating.

All the energy used in data centers produces enormous quantities of greenhouse gases.

What Are the Effects of Climate Change?

Warming temperatures are causing heat waves and droughts. Too much heat can make some people sick.

A drought is a long period of time with no rain or less rainfall than usual.

Crops dying in dry land

Droughts cause water shortages, making it hard for farmers to grow crops and raise animals.

Wild animals struggle to find enough water and food during droughts.

Earth's water cycle is changing. How?

More water on Earth is evaporating because of warmer temperatures. Eventually, it falls back to Earth as rain.

However, all this extra rain is mostly falling in places that already get plenty of rain. It's not falling in dry areas where people need water!

How The Water Cycle Works

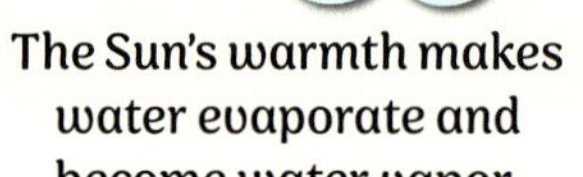

The water vapor cools and becomes water droplets in clouds.

The water droplets fall back to Earth as rain.

More rainfall can make rivers overflow. This can cause flooding to nearby homes.

As Earth warms up, climate scientists think that extreme storms, such as hurricanes and typhoons, could become more powerful. This may cause floods and damage to wild habitats and people's homes.

Is climate change causing the forest fires we see on the news?

No! Climate change doesn't cause forest fires. More than 80 percent of wildfires in the United States are started by people.

Some fires are deliberately started by people.

However, warming temperatures can make wildfires worse.

During long periods of dry weather, trees and other plants dry out and die. Dead branches, leaves, and other material on the forest floor get drier.

Dry plant material on forest floor

Camp fires, cigarettes, and backyard bonfires can start wildfires.

Sparks from machines, vehicles, and power cables cause fires.

Once a fire starts, there is plenty of fuel to burn! The dry conditions help the fire spread more easily and burn for longer.

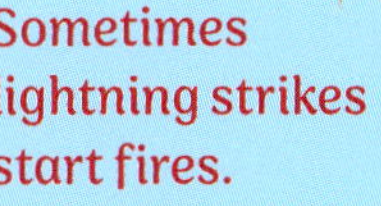

Sometimes lightning strikes start fires.

Are the North and South Poles Melting?

Earth's warming temperature is melting ice in the Arctic (North Pole) and Antarctica (South Pole).

The Arctic (North Pole)

North America

South America

The polar, or Arctic, ice cap is a vast floating island of frozen seawater.

During autumn and winter, more water freezes and the ice cap grows bigger. In spring and summer, ice melts and the ice cap gets smaller.

Arctic Ice Cap

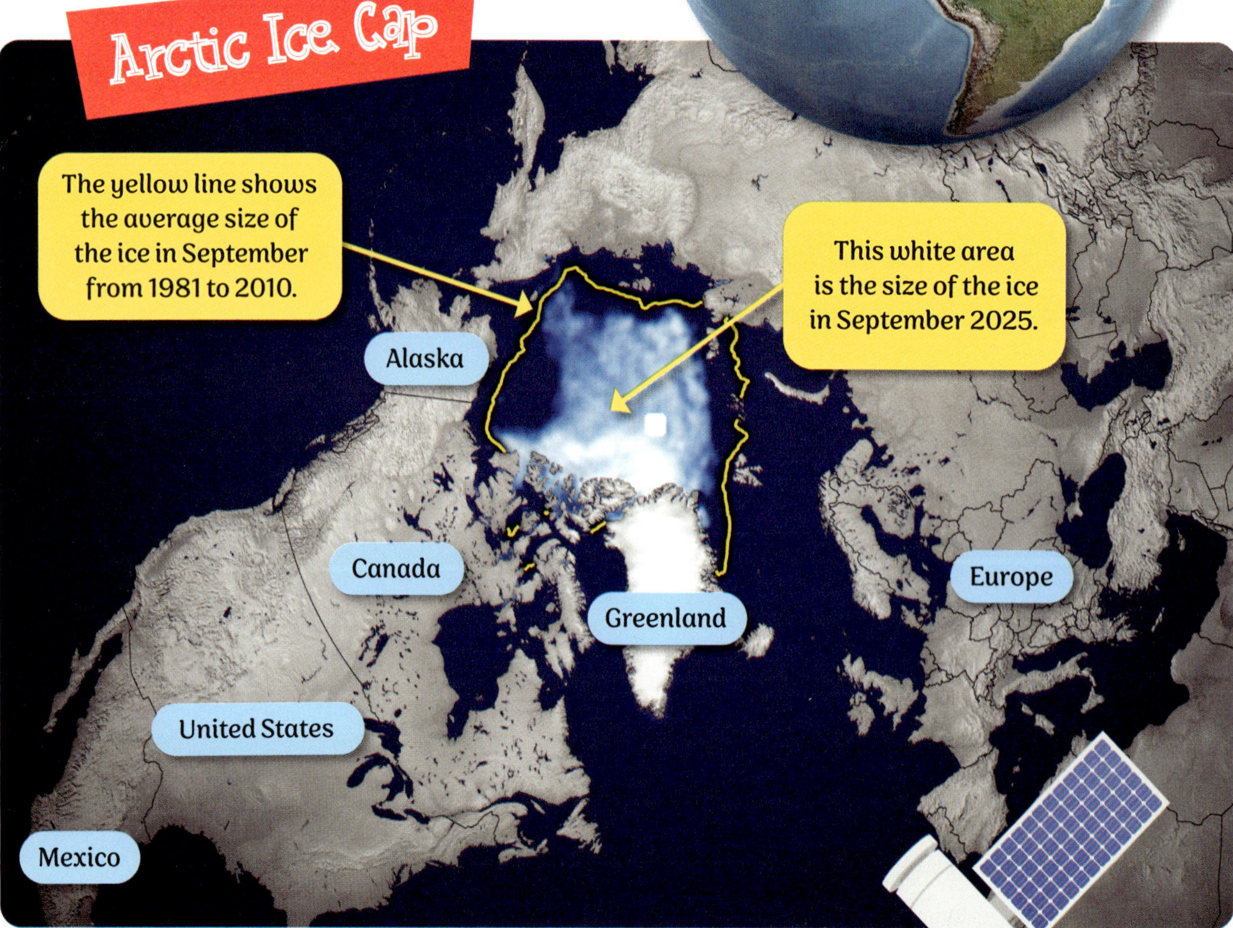

Satellite images now show that each summer, more ice melts. And in winter, less new ice forms.

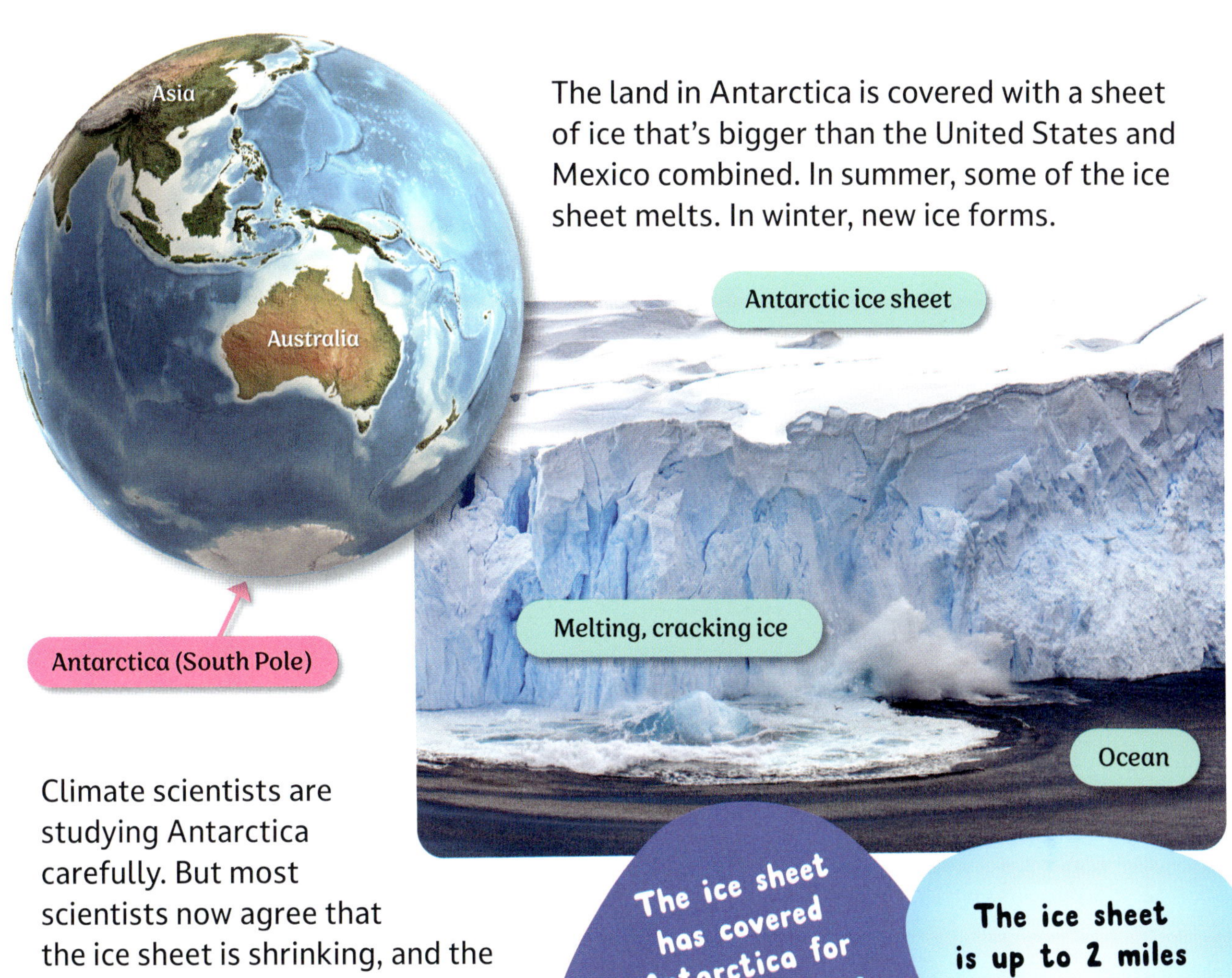

The land in Antarctica is covered with a sheet of ice that's bigger than the United States and Mexico combined. In summer, some of the ice sheet melts. In winter, new ice forms.

Climate scientists are studying Antarctica carefully. But most scientists now agree that the ice sheet is shrinking, and the amount of melting is speeding up!

The ice sheet has covered Antarctica for 30 million years.

The ice sheet is up to 2 miles (3.2 km) thick.

Climate change is causing sea levels to rise.

Why?

AS WATER IN EARTH'S SEAS GETS WARMER, IT EXPANDS. THIS MAKES SEA LEVELS RISE.

WATER FROM MELTING ICE SHEETS IN ANTARCTICA AND GREENLAND FLOWS INTO THE OCEAN.

MELTING ICE FROM MOUNTAINS FLOWS INTO RIVERS AND OUT TO SEA.

People who live near coastlines or on flat islands are worried that their homes will eventually be flooded.

Since 1880, Earth's sea levels have risen by about 10 inches (25 cm).

Will Climate Change Cause Animal Extinctions?

Earth's warming temperature is making survival harder for some animals.

Polar Bears

Polar bears hunt for seals on the floating Arctic sea ice. They also find mates on the ice, and female bears dig dens where they give birth to their cubs. Less Arctic sea ice is making it harder for polar bears to find food and raise their young.

Polar bears catch seals when they come to the surface to breathe at holes and cracks in the ice.

Emperor Penguins

Emperor penguins lay their eggs and raise their chicks on large areas of sea ice attached to the shores of Antarctica. Most emperor penguin colonies return to the same area to breed each year. As ice in Antarctica reduces, some colonies are losing their breeding grounds.

Emperor penguin adults and chicks

Competition for Food

In Canada, red foxes that used to live in the warmer south are moving north into the Arctic region. They compete for prey with the Arctic fox that has always lived in this habitat. The larger red foxes can drive the little Arctic foxes from their hunting grounds or even kill and eat them.

Insects in Danger

Earth's warming climate could create problems for insects.

- Droughts may kill the plants that insects feed on.
- Floods, wildfires, and extreme weather events kill insects and destroy their nests.
- Insects are part of almost all food chains on land. If their numbers go down, it affects birds and other animals that feed on insects.

Pressures on Pollinators

Queen bumblebees hibernate until early spring. When they wake up, they urgently need to feed on nectar from spring flowers before they can start laying eggs to form a new colony. However, warmer weather may cause some spring flowers to appear early. By the time the bees are awake, the flowers might have died.

It's Not Only Climate Change!

The biggest danger that most wild animals face today is actually habitat loss. Tropical rain forests, wild meadows, old woodlands, and wetlands are destroyed to create farmland, new roads, shopping malls, homes, and other buildings.

Around the world, scientists and conservationists are tracking wild animal numbers and studying the ways that human actions are affecting them.

Finding ways to protect natural habitats and slow down global warming will help keep wild animals safe.

How Do Scientists Study and Track Climate Change?

Thousands of scientists around the world have been studying Earth's atmosphere, climate, weather, oceans, and land for decades!

Carbon Dioxide Levels

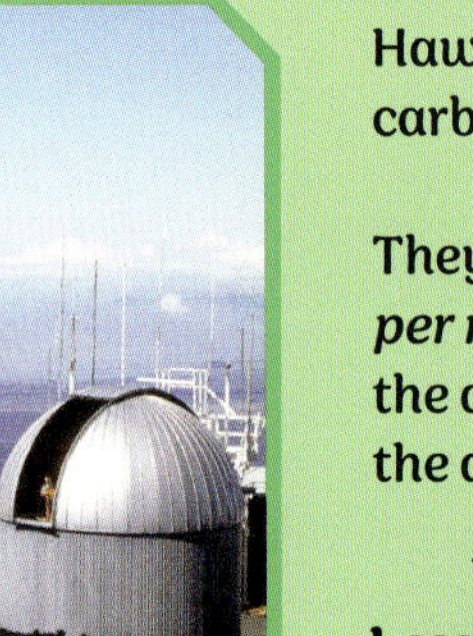

Mauna Loa Research Station

At a research station on a volcano in Hawaii, climate scientists measure carbon dioxide in the atmosphere.

They use a measurement called *parts per million* (ppm). Their work shows the amount of this greenhouse gas in the air has increased.

Year: 1960	Year: 2025
Less than 320 ppm	425 ppm

Sea Levels

Satellites launched by NASA (National Aeronautics and Space Administration) and ESA (European Space Agency) measure sea levels from space. Their measurements track how sea levels are changing.

Copernicus Sentinel-6B satellite orbiting Earth

All Earth's oceans and seas are measured every 10 days.

Sea levels are rising by about 1/8 inch (3.3 mm) each year.

Ice Core Data

In Antarctica, scientists drill cores of ice from deep inside the ice sheet. Some of the ice is up to 800,000 years old.

There are ancient air bubbles trapped in the ice. Scientists test this air from thousands of years ago for greenhouse gases.

Their tests show that greenhouse gases were lower in Earth's past, and have risen in the last 100 years.

Scientists drilling for ice cores

An ice core is 3 feet (1 m) long.

Measuring Temperatures

When Earth has so many different temperatures, how do we know Earth's average temperature has risen by 2.2°F (1.2°C)?

Every year, billions of temperature measurements are taken worldwide. Scientists use this data, computer programs, and lots of complicated science and math to calculate an average amount. But it works a little like this:

Place 1	**Place 2**	**Place 3**	**Place 4**
Warmed by 3 degrees	Warmed by 2.8 degrees	Warmed by 1 degree	Warmed by 2 degrees

3 + 2.8 + 1 + 2 = 8.8 degrees
The total is divided by the four places.
8.8 ÷ 4 = 2.2 degrees average warming

Scientists have been measuring temperatures around the world for about 150 years.

All the scientists' results agree. Human actions are creating more greenhouse gases, and Earth is warming up!

How Do I Know What Information to Trust?

Sometimes the things we see, hear, and read online about climate change are worrying or confusing.

Humans will be extinct in 10 years!

Our planet is dying. There will be no food by 2030.

The above statements aren't true. So, when you see information like this, ask yourself these questions:

Who is saying this? Are they a scientist? Or are they someone who wants me to share their post?

What scientific evidence are they showing me?

Do scientists agree with this person? Do your own research using books and reliable websites, such as NASA's. Ask a teacher or another adult to help you.

Does the video or post include spooky music or disaster-movie-type images? Has it been created to inform you, or scare and panic you?

Does the video or post include a doom countdown, such as "5 years to save the planet"? Real scientists never make scary predictions like this.

Why do some people say fake things about climate change?

A person might read something online that's not true. Then algorithms show them more of this information. It starts to feel real.

It might feel better to pretend something scary is not happening.

People worry that changing how we live to slow down global warming will be expensive or they might lose their jobs.

If one winter is colder than usual, someone might think global warming isn't happening. But this is short-term weather—it's not long-term climate change.

Sometimes people misunderstand information. They get scared or confused.

Some people might say untrue things to get a bigger audience or more followers. Algorithms are more likely to share and spread posts and videos that are shocking and scary.

More clicks may mean the person earns more money.

A person might want to feel special or get a reputation for knowing secret stuff—even if it's wrong.

Every scientific organization around the world agrees climate change is happening. But our world isn't going to end. And the fight back to care for our planet is underway.

Can We Still Power Our World While Making Fewer Greenhouse Gases?

Yes! Scientists and engineers have given us planet-friendly ways to produce electricity, such as wind and solar power.

These ways to make energy are renewable and won't run out. And they produce fewer greenhouse gases than burning fossil fuels in power stations.

Renewable Energy from Water

At a hydroelectric power station, water in a river builds up behind a dam. It forms a reservoir, or lake. When the water is released through the dam, it rushes past machines called turbines, making them spin. The spinning turbines turn a generator that makes electricity.

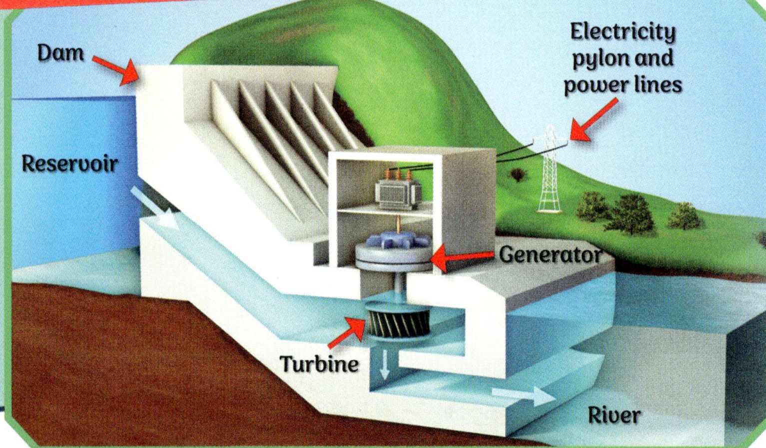

Renewable Energy from Waste

Food waste that's collected from homes, shops, and restaurants can be used to make energy. So can animal and plant waste from farms. This waste, called biomass, is put into an anaerobic digester. Microbes inside the digester break down the waste and convert it into biogas.

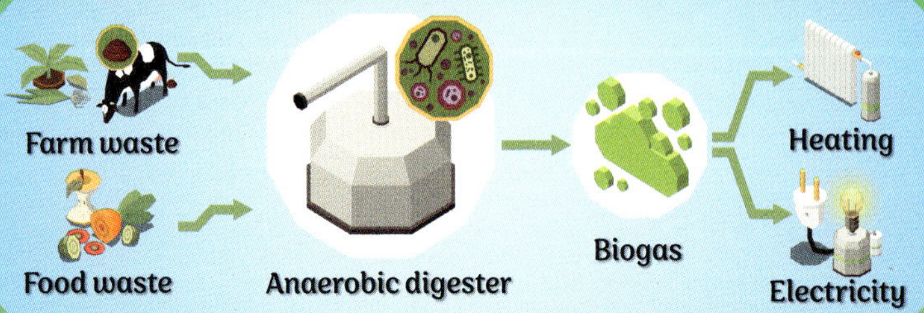

The biogas can be used to heat buildings or as fuel to power electricity plants. Biogas produces fewer greenhouse gases than burning fossil fuels.

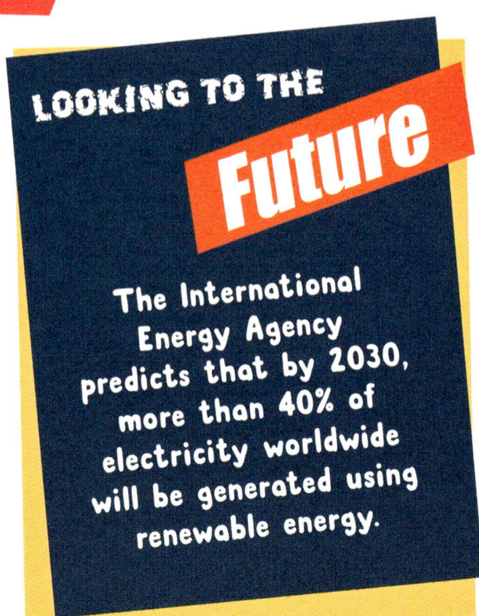

LOOKING TO THE Future

The International Energy Agency predicts that by 2030, more than 40% of electricity worldwide will be generated using renewable energy.

Planet-Friendly Electric Travel

Some cars, buses, and other vehicles are powered by electricity rather than gasoline or diesel fuels that produce lots of greenhouse gases. Using electric vehicles will help reduce greenhouse gases. But only as long as the electricity is generated using renewable energy sources.

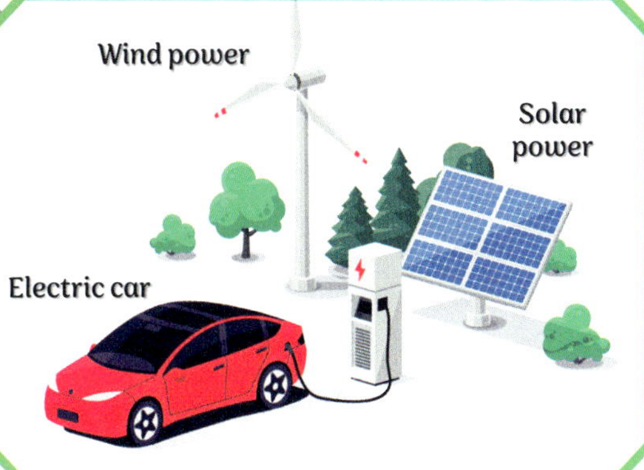

Recycling Data Center Heat

Remember all that unwanted heat that's produced by computers in data centers? In some places, engineers have invented and built machines that capture the heat. Then it is delivered through underground pipes to heat nearby homes, schools, and other buildings.

Recycling data center heat means homes and other buildings use less natural gas and electricity for heating, which creates fewer greenhouse gases.

Waste Heat to Electricity

Big factories make things we use every day, such as steel, cement, and glass. Inside these factories, it gets very hot. About 60% of that heat goes to waste. A company called ATS Energy found a smart way to use that wasted heat.

Making steel

Energy cartridge

ATS Energy makes special energy cartridges that turn leftover heat into clean electricity. At a factory, many energy cartridges are connected together. The factory's heat is channeled to the cartridges. When heat flows through the cartridges, they make electricity with no pollution. Factories can make their own clean power while saving money, energy, and the environment!

Can We Take Carbon Dioxide Out of the Air?

Our planet already has ways to keep the amount of carbon dioxide in the air balanced.

However, these natural processes can't keep up with the extra carbon dioxide produced by human activities.

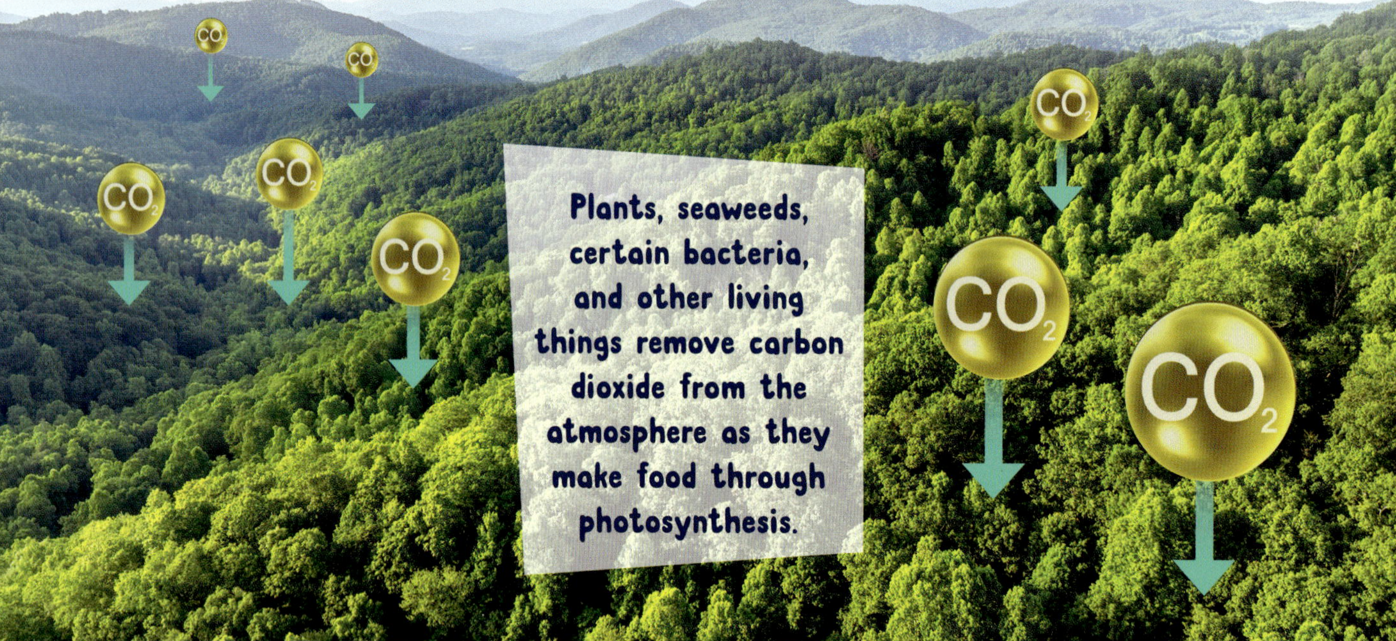

Plants, seaweeds, certain bacteria, and other living things remove carbon dioxide from the atmosphere as they make food through photosynthesis.

Trapping Gases in Rock

Scientists and engineers are working on ways to take carbon dioxide gas from the atmosphere and turn it into solid rock!

Special machines capture carbon dioxide and dissolve it in water. The liquid becomes a little like fizzy soda. Next the fizzy liquid is pumped deep underground into porous (hole-filled) rocks, such as basalt. Chemical reactions take place and the gas mineralizes and becomes chalky rock, filling the holes in the basalt.

Carbon dioxide gas

Porous basalt rock

Basalt

Mineralized carbon dioxide

This process happens naturally, but it takes thousands or millions of years. Scientists hope they can turn carbon dioxide into rock and trap it underground in less than two years!

Recycling Waste Gases

From shampoo bottles to stretchy sportswear, we make lots of things with plastic. Most plastics are made from oil. Now, scientists are developing ways to turn waste gases from factories and landfill sites into plastics.

The gases, which include carbon dioxide, are fed into a tank called a bioreactor. Inside the bioreactor, microbes feed on the gases and produce waste. Their waste is a very useful product called ethanol.

Waste gases

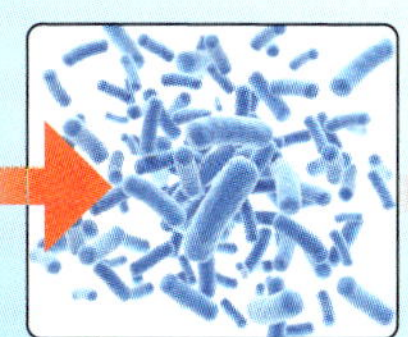

Recycling microbes

New products

Extracting oil from underground and turning it into plastic creates large amounts of greenhouse gases.

Ethanol can be turned into materials that are used to make packaging, clothing, and many other products.

Adapting to Climate Change

On the southern coast of Bangladesh, the land is flat. When a storm hits, millions of people are in danger from ocean floodwaters. An organization called "Friendship" is helping coastal communities be ready for the effects of climate change.

Working with local people, Friendship is planting mangrove forests on the coast. The forests act like a barrier, slowing down powerful waves and helping hold back floodwaters.

The trees' leaves will take carbon dioxide from the air.

Mangrove trees have special roots that can live in salty water.

There are many ways we can help remove greenhouse gases from the atmosphere. But it is VERY IMPORTANT that we also keep reducing the amount of these gases we produce.

Are There Other Ways to Reduce Greenhouse Gases?

Yes! All over the world, people are using their creativity and ingenuity to help protect our planet.

Recycling E-Waste

It's important that we recycle e-waste, such as old cell phones. To get metals, such as gold, silver, and copper, from these devices, the waste is crushed and heated at high temperatures. The metals melt and can be separated from the plastics and other materials.

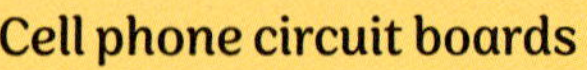
Cell phone circuit boards

Recycling metals uses less energy than mining new metals. However, it still creates greenhouse gases.

Scientists at the UK Royal Mint (where coins are made) have developed a new way to extract gold from old circuit boards.

Circuit board — Secret solution — Solid gold

Circuit boards are placed in a special green chemical solution. The gold dissolves into the liquid. Then, when another chemical is added to the liquid, the gold becomes solid metal again.

The scientists hope this process could one day be used to remove other metals from e-waste—without using large amounts of energy!

What's in the chemical solution is currently top secret!

At the 2020 Tokyo Olympics (held in 2021), the medals were made from recycled gold, silver, and bronze from e-waste. People across Japan donated old devices, including more than 6 million cell phones.

Greenhouse Gases from Cows?

Each year, billions of cattle and sheep are raised for meat and milk. As these animals digest grass and other food, they produce methane in their stomachs—lots of methane! This greenhouse gas is then released into the air.

Red Asparagopsis seaweed

Growing the seaweed will also help take carbon dioxide out of the air, because seaweeds photosynthesize, just like land plants.

In Australia, scientists and business people have developed a food supplement made from a type of red seaweed. Just a small amount in an animal's feed cuts its methane production by up to 90%!

From Garbage to Concrete

We need concrete to build everything around us from homes to roads. Concrete is made from cement, sand, water, and small stones called aggregates.

Aggregates

The machines that dig aggregates from rock quarries and the trucks that transport them produce big quantities of greenhouse gases.

Digging for aggregates

A team of British university students have developed a new type of aggregate that can be used in construction. Their invention is made from garbage that can't be recycled! This waste would have been burned, creating even more greenhouse gases.

What Can I Do to Help?

Around the world, people are doing amazing things to slow down global warming and protect our planet. You can take action and help, too!

Take shorter showers to save energy and water.

Switch off lights to save energy!

CHOOSE CLOTHES, SHAMPOO, SHOWER GEL, DRINKS, SNACKS, AND OTHER PRODUCTS THAT ARE MADE BY COMPANIES THAT ARE TRYING TO PROTECT WILD HABITATS AND REDUCE THEIR ENERGY USE AND WASTE.

ALWAYS RECYCLE!

Join or start an eco-club at your school so you can work with friends on recycling, waste reduction, and energy-saving projects.

Walk or cycle instead of using the car.

MAKING NEW CLOTHES AND SHOES USES HUGE AMOUNTS OF ENERGY. TRY TO BUY PRELOVED ITEMS. SELL ONLINE OR DONATE YOUR UNWANTED CLOTHES TO A CHARITY. DON'T THROW THEM AWAY.

Lots of energy is used on farms, in factories, by trucks, in stores, and in kitchens to put food on your plate. Eat up and don't waste food! If you can recycle food waste with your garbage collectors, always do this. Then the waste could become renewable, planet-friendly energy (see page 22).

Celebrate the Wins!

Share the facts, positive stories, and tips you've read in this book. Tell two friends what you've learned. If they both tell two people, the good news will spread!

Could YOU Change the Future?

Many of the scientists, engineers, and entrepreneurs who are helping protect our planet from climate change are just a few years older than you! So enjoy your science lessons. Maybe one day you could invent a new, renewable way to power our homes? Or discover a way to help crops withstand drought?

Be a Habitat Creator

Plants mean food and homes for wild animals. They also take carbon dioxide out of the air and make the oxygen we need to breathe.

- Say NO to plastic grass. Real grass fights climate change and is a home for our smallest wildlife.
- You can grow plants in a small corner of a backyard, a window box, or even a flowerpot on a balcony.
- Plant a tree.

Save e-Energy and Reduce e-Waste!

- Unplug devices and chargers when not in use.
- Make sure energy-saving settings are being used on your devices.
- Buy refurbished, pre-owned tech instead of new.
- Resell old devices.
- Always recycle old or damaged tech.

Get Ready to Vote

When there's an election, go online and read what the different political parties will do to protect wild animals and habitats, make renewable energy more available and cheaper to buy, support businesses that have planet-friendly ideas, and help people worldwide live better, safer lives. You may not be able to vote yet. BUT GET READY!

Is It Too Late to Fix Our Planet?

No! As you've seen in this book, there is lots of good news.

Yes! And here are some reasons why:

- Every reduction in greenhouse gases helps.
- Reducing fossil fuel use keeps the air cleaner in your country.
- Your country can be an innovator. If it shows that new types of energy and technology work, other countries will want them, too.
- Planet-friendly businesses in your country can sell their inventions or ideas to other countries.
- Poorer countries may take longer to make the switch. The things your country does will be a guide they can follow.
- Being a leader is a good thing.

A Better World for Everyone

We need to find ways for people everywhere to improve their lives while using energy that produces fewer greenhouse gases.

Good News!

In the last 100 years, deaths when natural disasters strike, such as earthquakes, floods, hurricanes, and droughts, have dropped by 90%. Why? Humans have adapted and invented ways to make life better and safer.

- Stronger buildings that can withstand disasters.
- Barriers and other ways to hold back floods.
- Satellites and other equipment that track weather and predict disasters.
- Radios, cell phones, the internet, and other systems that inform and warn people of dangers.
- Better emergency healthcare.

People will continue to invent and adapt in order to live with climate change.

HERE ARE SOME IMPORTANT FINAL THINGS TO REMEMBER.

Remember! People around the world already live in very different climates. They survive in the freezing Arctic and in dry, hot deserts. Humans are very good at adapting how we live to suit different climates.

MILLIONS OF PEOPLE AROUND THE WORLD ARE DOING POSITIVE THINGS TO HELP.

RENEWABLE ENERGY USE IS GROWING WORLDWIDE.

Our future is filled with hope!

GLOSSARY

carbon dioxide
A colorless gas in the atmosphere. Its chemical symbol is CO_2, which shows it is made of one carbon atom (C) and two oxygen atoms (O_2).

climate
The usual weather and temperatures in an area over a long period of time.

climate change
The way in which Earth's climate changes over time.

fossil fuels
Sources of energy (oil, coal, and natural gas) made of carbon. They formed over millions of years from the fossilized remains of dead prehistoric plants and animals.

global warming
The gradual increase (over many decades) of temperatures on Earth.

greenhouse gases
The gases (carbon dioxide, water vapor, and methane) that trap heat in Earth's atmosphere.

photosynthesis
The process by which plants and some other living things make food using water, carbon dioxide, and sunlight.

renewable energy
Energy from natural sources, such as wind, water, and the Sun, that will never run out.

weather
The temperature and conditions, such as rain or wind, in an area over a short period of time.

INDEX

A

animals 4–5, 7, 12, 16–17, 22, 27, 29

Arctic and Antarctica 7, 14–15, 16–17, 19, 31

C

carbon dioxide capture 24–25

climate change effects 4–5, 7, 8–9, 12–13, 14–15, 16–17, 25

climate (what is it?) 6

F

fossil fuels 9, 10, 22, 30

G

greenhouse gases 8–9, 10–11, 12–13, 18–19, 22–23, 24–25, 26–27, 30

O

oceans 4, 15, 18, 25

online information 5, 11, 20–21

P

positive actions to help 4–5, 18–19, 22–23, 24–25, 26–27, 28–29, 30–31

R

renewable energy 22–23, 29, 31

W

weather 4–5, 6, 12–13, 17, 18, 21, 25, 31